The Unofficial Guide to the Afterlife

Text © Ziggy Hanaor and Laura Winstone
Illustration © Laura Winstone
Design by Ben Javens

British Library Cataloguing-in-Publication Data.

A CIP record for this book is available from the British Library
ISBN: 978-1-80066-012-0

First published in 2022

Cicada Books Ltd
48 Burghley Road
London, NW5 1UE
www.cicadabooks.co.uk

Printed in Poland

THE ~~UN~~OFFICIAL GUIDE TO THE ANCIENT EGYPTIAN AFTERLIFE

AFTERLIFE TOUR STARTS HERE

Bastet

Before we set off, I'll just tell you a bit about myself. As a cat, I'm kind of a big deal here in Egypt. We cats chase mice out of the grain stores and kill the occasional scorpion, and in return we are treated as gods.

When a cat dies, its owner shaves off their eyebrows and howls in grief. You can actually be put to death for killing a cat.

My pre-death career was as the Pharaoh's cat. As you can imagine, it was a very stressful job. I was laden with jewels and fed only the most delicious morsels of meat.

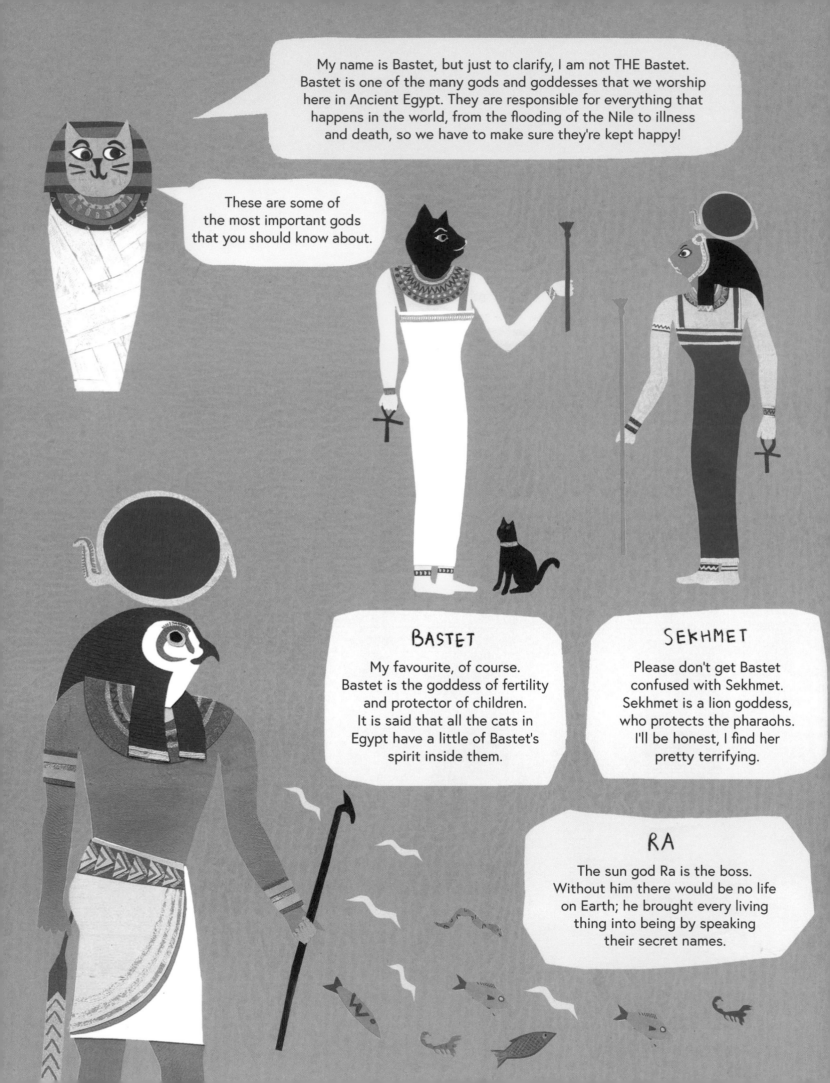

Osiris wears the Atef Crown,
decorated with ostrich feathers.

Isis wears a crown of cow
horns and a solar disc,
representing the sun.

OSIRIS

Osiris is the second most important of
the gods. He was the ruler of Egypt until
his nasty brother, Set, stole the throne,
killed him and chopped him up into little
bits. His wife, Isis, hunted down all the
pieces and mummified him so that he
could pass through to the afterlife, where
he became king of the dead.

ISIS

Isis is Osiris's wife as well
as his sister (strange, I know).
She is the goddess of
motherhood, protection,
healing and magic.

You can tell Osiris is dead
because his skin is green.

Horus wears the Pschent Crown,
which combines the Red Crown of
Lower Egypt with the White Crown
of Upper Egypt.

HORUS

Horus is the son of Isis and Osiris.
He is god of the sky and protector
of Egypt. After a long, bloody battle,
in which he lost an eye, Horus
managed to kill his evil uncle
Set and reclaim the throne. Horus
has the head of a hawk. He flies
across the sky every evening and
morning, turning day into night and
back again.

After the great battles of Osiris, Set and Horus, the gods decided to leave
the ruling of Egypt to humans. The pharaohs are the spokespeople of the gods.
They own all the land, make all the laws and maintain *maat*, or cosmic order.

The word pharaoh
means 'great house'.

Only the pharaoh is allowed to wear the
cobra crown. It is protected by a cobra
goddess who spits flames.

When a pharaoh dies, it is a time
of great mourning for the whole country.
When my owner died, I could see things were
going to get bad for me pretty quickly. Cats are
lucky, and the pharaoh needs all the luck he can
get in the afterlife...

QEBEHSENUEF

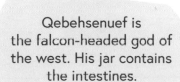

Canopic jars are made of stone or pottery. The top of each jar is carved in the shape of the head of one of the four sons of Horus.

IMSETY

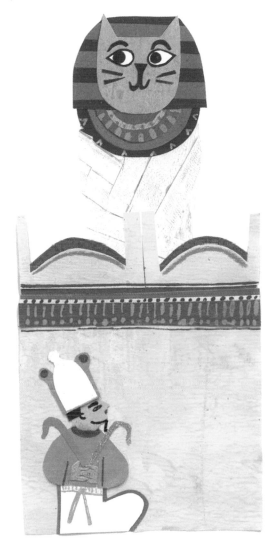

Qebehsenuef is the falcon-headed god of the west. His jar contains the intestines.

Imsety is the human-headed goddess of the south. She looks after the liver.

DUAMUTEF

HAPI

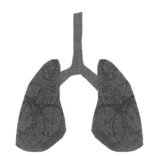

Duamutef is the jackal-headed god of the east. He guards the stomach.

Hapi is the baboon-headed goddess of the north. She guards the lungs.

The sarcophagi are often decorated with eyes, so the person can see out.

EYE OF HORUS

The most important eye symbol is the Eye of Horus. As you recall, the god Horus had a terrible battle with his evil uncle Set, who stole the throne from Horus's dad, Osiris. Horus's eye was wounded in battle, but it was healed by the god of learning, Thoth. Horus then gave this eye to his father, and its power sustained Osiris in the afterlife.

The eye of Horus represents healing and regeneration, as well as generosity and appeasement of the gods. It is one of the most protective magical symbols in all of Ancient Egypt.

CARTOUCHE

This says 'Bastet' in hieroglyphics. You'll learn more about those later...

You'll also see a rope symbol on the sarcophagi. This is a cartouche. It protects whatever words are written inside it. Your true name is called your 'ren', and as long as your ren is protected, you can live forever in the afterlife. So you must always protect your name inside a cartouche!

These are some other magical symbols that we use to decorate the sarcophagus.

LOTUS FLOWER
symbolises rebirth.

CROOK
symbolises the Pharaoh's role as shepherd of the people.

NTJR
an axe that represents godliness.

WAS SCEPTRE
an animal-headed sceptre symbolising godly power.

ANKH
represents eternal life.

OUROBOROS
a snake that eats its own tail, representing eternity.

FLAIL
a rod with three strands of beads representing kingship and order.

DJED
a column, which symbolises stability.

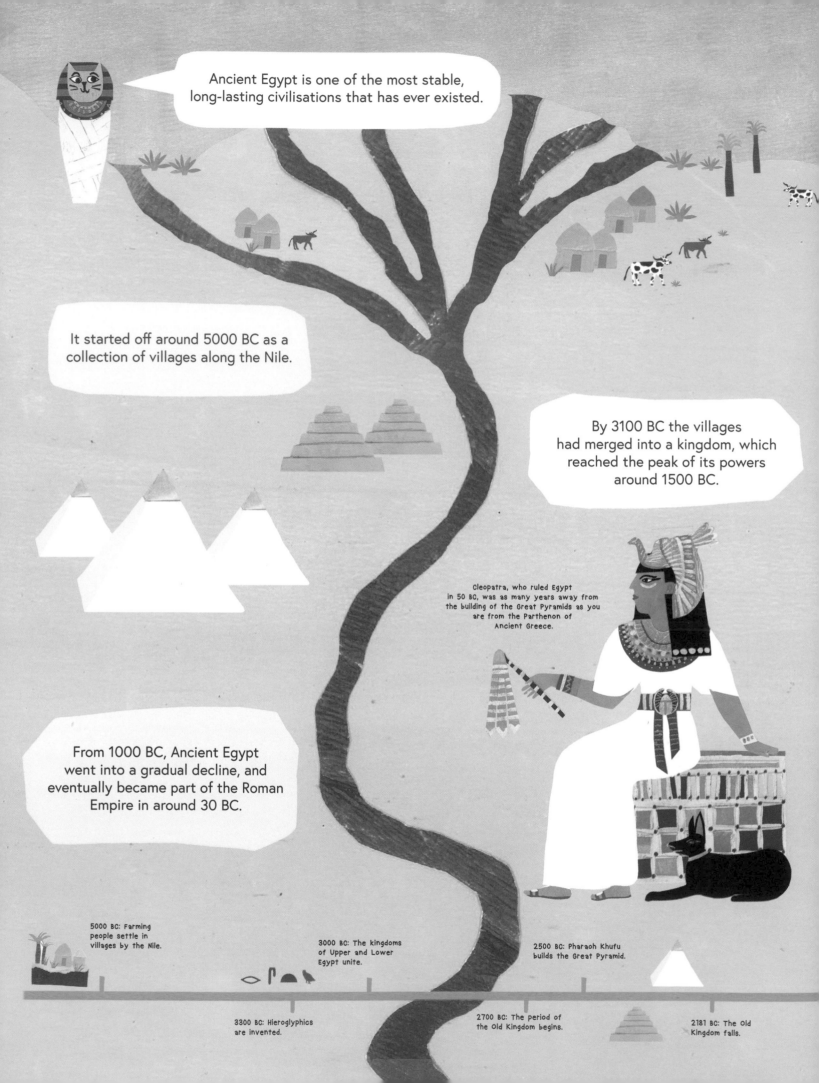

Now, as you might expect, there were some changes in the way things were done during this incredibly long history. To begin with, pharaohs were buried in tombs called mastabas. These were simple, rectangular stone rooms with an underground chamber, where the body was kept.

MASTABA

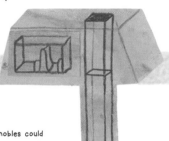

Only pharaohs and wealthy nobles could afford tombs like these. Commoners were buried in the sand using a much simpler form of mummification.

Djoser's Pyramid was the first massive tomb, standing 60 metres tall.

This is Imhotep, the architect of Djoser's Pyramid.

Gradually, the mastabas began to grow. In 2670 BC, Pharaoh Djoser designed the first stepped pyramid. It had six layers, representing the Pharaoh's stepladder to heaven.

Saqqara is an ancient necropolis (which means a 'city of the dead'). As well as Djoser's Pyramid, it contains 15 other pyramids along with many treasures of the Old Kingdom.

2055 BC: The Middle Kingdom; a period of artistic achievement.

1550 BC: The New Kingdom; a period of conquest and power.

664 BC: The Late Period; Egypt is conquered by various foreign powers.

332 BC: Alexander the Great takes control.

51 BC: Queen Cleopatra is the last ruler of Ancient Egypt.

30 BC: The Romans conquer. Ancient Egypt is defeated.

Djoser's stepped pyramid design was so popular, soon everyone wanted one! The steps began to be smoothed over and the pyramids started to look the way you probably imagine them.

These are the Great Pyramids of Giza, vast tombs built for the pharaohs of the Fourth Dynasty. The biggest is Khufu's Pyramid, built in 2500 BC. It measures 140 metres tall – the size of 28 stacked double decker busses! It took only 25 years to build.

Archaeologists believe that when they were first built, the pyramids were clad in white limestone and had a golden tip that shone out across the desert.

Standing guard over the pyramids is this fine Sphynx, which was carved directly into the bedrock. He has the face of one of the most famous and successful pharaohs, Pharaoh Khafre, and the body of a giant cat. Lucky chap!

By the time of the New Kingdom
in 1500 BC, many of the Old Kingdom
pyramids had been looted for their gold
and treasures, and nobles chose instead
to be buried in secret tombs in the cliffs at
the edge of the Western Desert. This area
is known as the Valley of the Kings. It
contains 64 tombs and burial chambers.

Unfortunately, the tombs in the Valley of the Kings were also eventually raided,
except for the tomb of the boy king, Tutankhamun. This was a smaller tomb,
partly hidden by rubble. It was discovered in 1922, filled with wonderful treasures
that give a taste of what the bigger tombs once contained.

Before you're put away in your tomb for good, everyone has a bit of a party. It's called the 'opening of the mouth ceremony'. All your friends and family follow the priests to the tomb, carrying grave goods and wailing a lot.

At the entrance to the tomb, your mummy is placed upright and a priest touches your mouth (or rather the painting of your mouth) with his special holy tools, allowing your spirit to pass into the afterlife.

After that, a great feast is laid out on a table outside the tomb. The priests say a magical spell that allows your Ka to be nourished by the food. Once that's done, they go and eat it themselves. How very rude.

I hope you're not expecting to be pampered in the afterlife. It's no picnic, you know. You need to make sure you take ALL your belongings with you when you leave this world behind.

In my owner's tomb we have food, tools, combs, clothes, furniture, jewellery, baskets and even boardgames. My favourite boardgame is Senet, which we invented way back in 3500 BC.

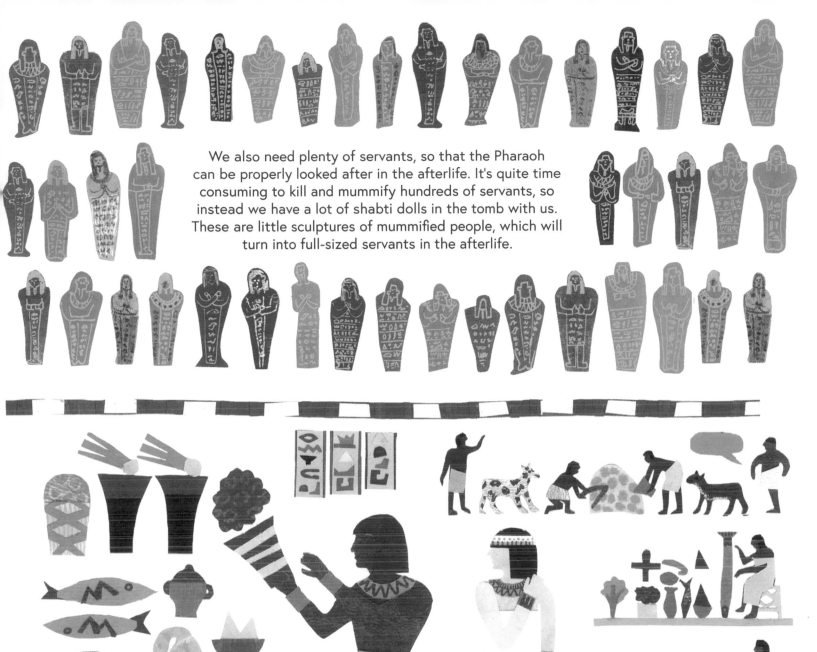

We also need plenty of servants, so that the Pharaoh can be properly looked after in the afterlife. It's quite time consuming to kill and mummify hundreds of servants, so instead we have a lot of shabti dolls in the tomb with us. These are little sculptures of mummified people, which will turn into full-sized servants in the afterlife.

You'll notice plenty of paintings on the walls of the tomb. This is because, like the shabti dolls, the pictures turn into reality once you pass through to the afterlife. Anything that is not painted is left behind. That is why pictures of people have all their limbs visible. If you don't draw both legs, you might reach the afterlife with just one!

Oh golly, I almost forgot!
Before you embark on the journey that lasts all eternity,
make sure you pack a copy of the Book of the Dead.

I'm not a great reader myself, but I'm told that these
scrolls hold all the passwords, spells and prayers to
get the soul through the mazes and obstacles that
line the way to the afterlife.

We Ancient Egyptians
write with symbols called hieroglyphics,
which are like tiny pictures that
represent letters.

This is Thoth,
god of learning.

There are over 700 of them,
none of which are vowel sounds,
so it's not an easy alphabet to master!

We believe that writing is the language of the
gods, and that words that are written down
have magical powers to capture
the object they describe.

Here's a simplified alphabet.

A B C D E F G

H H-CH I J K L M

N O P Q R S T U

V X Y Z TH

SH CH

Can you decipher the words in the cartouche?

The Book of the Dead is written on papyrus, which is an early form of paper made from the pulp of the papyrus plant. The sheets of papyrus are sewn together into a long scroll.

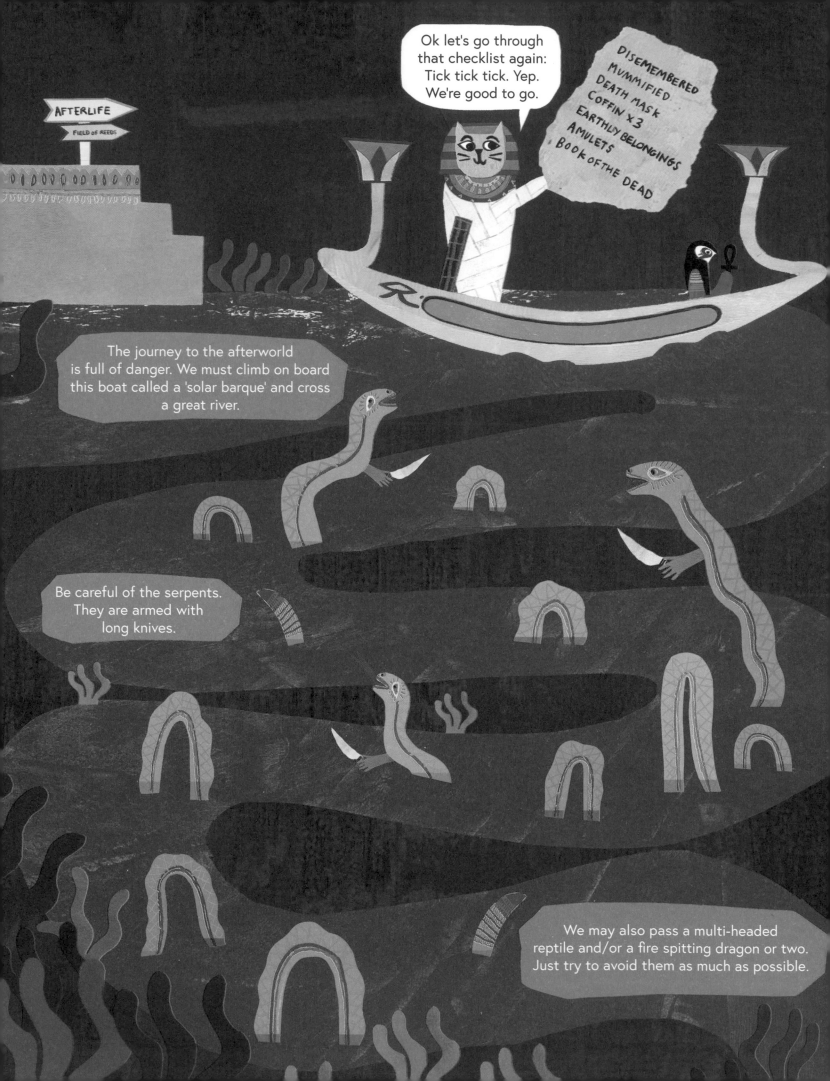

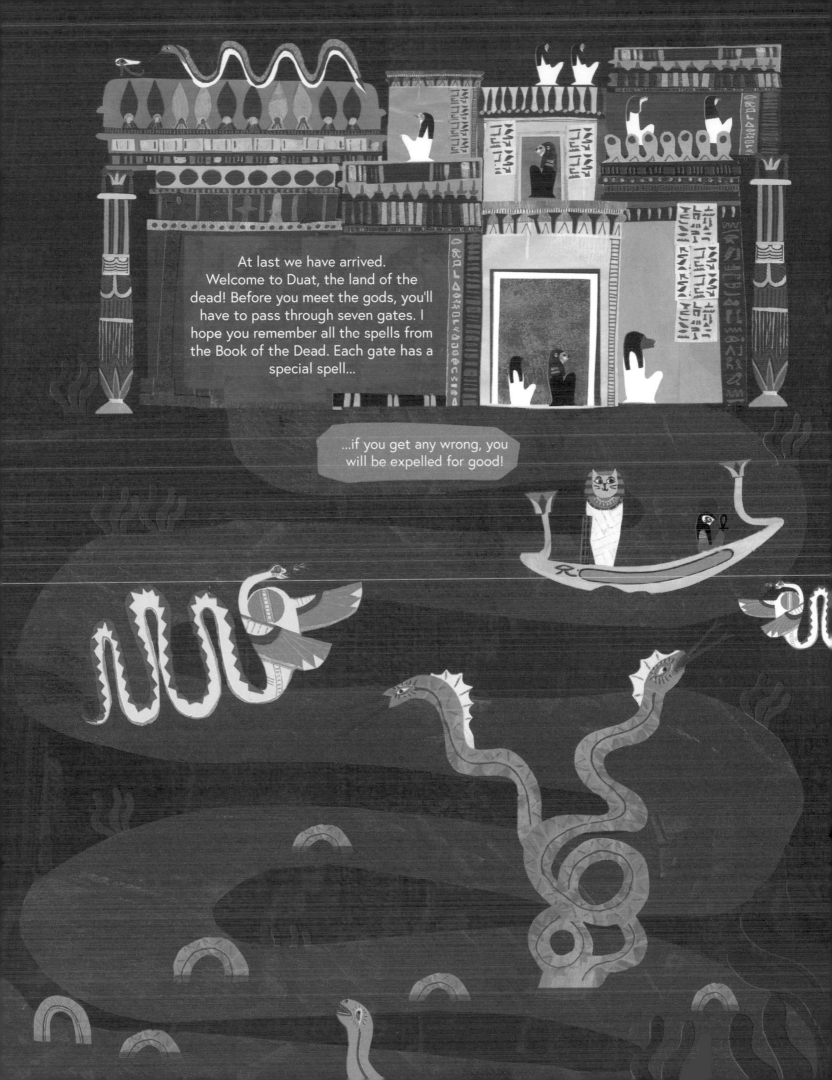

Well done, you made it through the gates. And now we have arrived at the Hall of Osiris, where you will be judged.

Yes, that's right, judged. Did I forget to tell you about this part? Oh whoops!

The god Anubis, here on the left with the jackal head, will oversee the weighing of your heart.

Start by confessing all your earthly sins to these 42 gods. You must identify them all correctly by their names or they'll take offense! After that, Anubis will take your heart and place it on a scale.

If it's as sinless as you say it is, it should counterbalance with the feather of Ma'at, goddess of truth and justice.

GLOSSARY

Amulet — A small, lucky object that offers protection. Amulets come in all shapes and colours, taking the form of animals, gods and symbols that represent rebirth, health, protection or eternity.

Anubis — The jackal-headed god of the dead, in charge of embalming and of ushering souls through to the afterlife.

Ba — The part of your soul that includes your personality; everything unique about you that is not physical. It is drawn as an eagle with a human head, and it can fly between the land of the living and the land of the dead.

Book of the Dead — A book of magical spells to protect you and help you navigate the long and difficult journey to the afterlife.

Canopic jars — Special pots used in the mummification process to look after your bodily organs; each decorated with the head of one of the four sons of Horus.

Cartouche — An elaborate rope frame decoration that protects whatever is written inside it.

Death mask — A mask placed on top of a mummy to help the Ba and Ka return to the correct body.

Djoser's Pyramid — A massive stepped pyramid built by Pharaoh Djoser in 2670 BC. It was the first monumental stone structure to be built in Ancient Egypt.

Duat — The land of the dead. It is divided into sections filled with dangers that the soul has to pass through to reach the afterlife beyond.

Eye of Horus — A powerful magical symbol that represents the eye of the god Horus, which was injured in battle and given to his father, Osiris, for protection in the afterlife.

Faience — A glazed ceramic with a bold colour (usually turquoise) as a result of special salts inside the clay.

Great Pyramids — A group of three enormous pyramids outside Cairo that were built for powerful pharaohs from the Old Kingdom.

Hall of Osiris — A hall of judgement in which the soul is weighed to determine whether it may pass through to the afterlife.

Hieroglyphics — The Ancient Egyptian alphabet, which consists of over 700 pictograms. It took historians many of hundreds of years to work out how to read them!

Horus — The falcon-headed god of kingship, power and healing.

Isis — Goddess of the moon, life, health and children. She is the daughter of Ra, the mother of Horus and wife and sister of Osiris.

Ka — Your life force. It is drawn as a pair of embracing arms.

Mastaba	A rectangular tomb structure with an underground burial chamber.
Middle Kingdom	Lasting from 2030 BC to 1650 BC, the Middle Kingdom was a time of stability and great artistic productivity.
Mummification	A way of preserving a dead body by drying it out or embalming it.
Natron	A type of salt that dries out the body very quickly.
New Kingdom	A period of power and expnansion. The Egyptian empire conquered lands south to today's Sudan and north to today's Lebanon. It lasted from 1550 BC to 1077 BC.
Nile	The river Nile was the life blood of Ancient Egypt, providing fertile soil for crops, a water source and a way of transporting goods for many miles.
Old Kingdom	The Old Kingdom was the era of pyramid building. It lasted from 2700 BC to 2130 BC.
Opening of the mouth ceremony	A ceremony in which a priest would touch a mummy's mouth so that it would be able to breathe, eat and speak in the afterlife.
Osiris	God of the underworld.
Papyrus	A type of paper made from the pulp of the papyrus plant.
Pharaoh	The ruler of Egypt, who was believed to be directly connected to the gods.
Ra	King of the gods and the father of all creation.
Saqqara	A great burial ground (necropolis) that was situated near the Ancient Egyptian capital, Memphis.
Sarcophagus	A stone coffin.
Scarabs	The scarab beetle or dung beetle lays its eggs inside animal poo, and the baby beetles then emerge fully formed. This was a powerful symbol of rebirth.
Sekhet-Aaru	Also known as Aaru; this is the heavenly 'field of reeds' ruled over by Osiris.
Shabti dolls	Amulets in the shape of a mummified humans that were thought to turn into servants in the afterlife.
Solar barque	A boat first used by Ra to carry souls through to the underworld.
Sphynx	A massive sculpture of a mythological beast with the body of a cat and the head of the Pharaoh Khafre.
Valley of the Kings	A valley on the west bank of the Nile, which contains 64 tombs of royal figures and nobles from the period of the New Kingdom.